WHALEWATCH!

WHALE WATCH!

By June Behrens

Photographs collected by John Olguin
Director, Cabrillo Marine Museum

A Golden Gate Junior Book   Childrens Press • Chicago

For the Monreal girls,
Ruth, Denise and Jennifer

ACKNOWLEDGEMENT

The author wishes to acknowledge with thanks the cooperation of
the NATIONAL GEOGRAPHIC SOCIETY

Cover:	National Geographic Photographer Bates Littlehales ©National Geographic Society
Title page:	National Geographic Photographer Bates Littlehales ©National Geographic Society
P. 19	Theodore J. Walker ©National Geographic Society
P. 22	Theodore J. Walker ©National Geographic Society
P. 25	National Geographic Photographer Bates Littlehales ©National Geographic Society

The following people assisted in the preparation of photography
for this manuscript:

Rafe Payne	Bill Philbin
Robert Bonde	Tom Thornton
Eda Rogers	

Special thanks go to the American Cetacean Society and the
Cabrillo Marine Museum volunteer guides for their assistance in
the development of this manuscript

Library of Congress Cataloging in Publication Data

Behrens, June.
  Whalewatch!

  "A Golden Gate junior book."
  SUMMARY: Text and photographs the experiences of
a group of school children on a whalewatch off the
California coast and what they learn about the habits
and behavior of the Pacific gray whale.
  1. Pacific gray whale--Juvenile literature.
(1. Pacific gray whale. 2. Whales) I. Olguin,
John. II. Title.
QL737.C425B43   599'.51   78-7338
ISBN 0-516-08873-4

WHALEWATCH!

IT'S Whalewatch Day!

Our school bus takes us to the Pacific Ocean.

We get on little whalewatch boats.

We ride offshore to see the winter migration of
      California gray whales.

Our guide knows all about whales.

We learn that it is important to protect and save
      our whales.

Not far from our boat we see a fountain-like spray.

It's our first whale!

Soon whales are all around us!

The guide says that on a good day boys and girls see as
      many as 50 whales.

Whales come to the top of the water to breathe.

When they breathe air out, we see spouts.

Spouting is sometimes called blowing.

Spouts look like a spraying fountain coming from the
   whale's head.

Some whales spout as high as 15 feet in the air.

From the Whalewatch boat we can see and hear a
   whale breathe.

His nose is on top of his head.

The nose has two holes, called blowholes.

When the whale breathes out through his blowholes,
   we hear a *whooshing* sound.

Whales live in the ocean but they are not fish.
They are called mammals.
They breathe air and are warm-blooded.
Whale babies, called calves, are born alive and drink
their mother's milk.
Whales are covered with skin and have some hair on
parts of their bodies.

Dolphins and porpoises are cousins of the whales.
They belong to a family called Cetacea.

11

Whales are the largest creatures living.
They are bigger than the biggest dinosaur that once
      walked the earth.
This gray whale died and washed ashore.
It is as long as our school bus.

California gray whales grow to 50 feet long and weigh
      up to 40 tons.
They are half the size of the giant blue whale!

We see white splotches on the whale's skin.
Barnacles and other sea animals live on the gray whales.

13

Look at that giant whale tail!

The two parts of the whale's tail are called flukes.

Flukes are sometimes 10 feet across.

These powerful flukes move up and down. They push
the whale through the water at high speeds.

Sometimes the whale uses his tail to protect himself
from his enemies.

"If whales are so heavy, why don't they sink to the
        bottom of the ocean?" one whalewatcher asked.
Our Whalewatch guide told us.
Whales have a coat of blubber under their skin. It is
        over a foot thick.
The blubber is lighter than water and helps the whale
        to float.
Blubber is the whale's stored food supply. It keeps the
        whale warm, like a diver's wet suit.

Years ago men killed the gray whales for their blubber.
They took oil from the blubber and sold it.
The whale population grew very small.
Today the whales are protected by laws.

Whales migrate south for the winter.
They travel with the change of seasons.

In summer the whales eat and grow fat in the
        cold waters near the Arctic.
Then, from December to February, we watch them
        swim down the Pacific coast.
They often travel in small groups of three or
        more, called pods.

Gray whales swim over 5,000 miles, from the Arctic
waters to the lagoons of Mexico. Their trip might
take them three months.

Our boat captain tells us that whales can hear for a
    long distance.
They use sound to help them navigate on their journey.
They use their ears to find other whales over three
    miles away.

We hear the whales "talking" around the boat!
Whale talk sounds like cries and whistles.
Whales grunt and make cracking sounds.

21

22

Whales take little naps several times a day
    on their long journey.
They might sleep for an hour at a time.
Whales nap on the surface of the water.
They bob their heads up about every five minutes
    to take a breath of air.

This baby is resting on its sleeping mother's back.
It weighs about half a ton and is just four hours old!
Do you see the baby whale's blowholes?

Our whalewatchers think whales are acrobats!
Sometimes they stick their heads out of the water and
look around.
This is called spyhopping.

Whales dive and splash the water with their tails.
It looks as though they are playing tag.

This whale is breaching.
He leaps out of the water, turns over and falls back
with a great splash.

24

26

Our gray whales will soon reach their winter home in
the warm lagoons of Mexico.

In the lagoons mothers will give birth to their
baby calves.
Babies sometimes weigh a ton and may be 15 feet long!
Female whales have babies every other year.

Whales mate and create new life in the warm lagoons.
They stay in their winter home from two to
three months.

In spring the herd of gray whales will move again.

In March and April we may see gray whales traveling
      north from Mexico.
They are on their way back to summer feeding grounds
      near the Arctic Ocean.

The gray whale herds travel more than 10,000 miles
      a year.
They make a round trip from the Arctic Ocean to
      Mexico and back again.

Some whales live to be 50 years old.
About how many miles have they migrated in their
      lifetime?
This seasonal move, or migration, is the longest made by
      any mammal.
Scientists think whales have been traveling this
      route for 8 million years.

THE CALIFORNIA GRAY WHALE

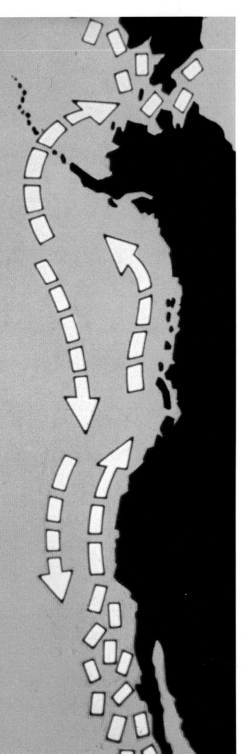

It has been a good whalewatch. We now know a lot
more about whales.

In June we will come back to the Pacific Ocean.
We will wear our bathing suits and bring our
sand shovels.
Each year whale lovers meet on the beach and make a
life-sized sand whale.

Expert whalewatchers believe that there are 11,000
California gray whales.
After our day on the beach there will be 11,001,
counting our sand whale.

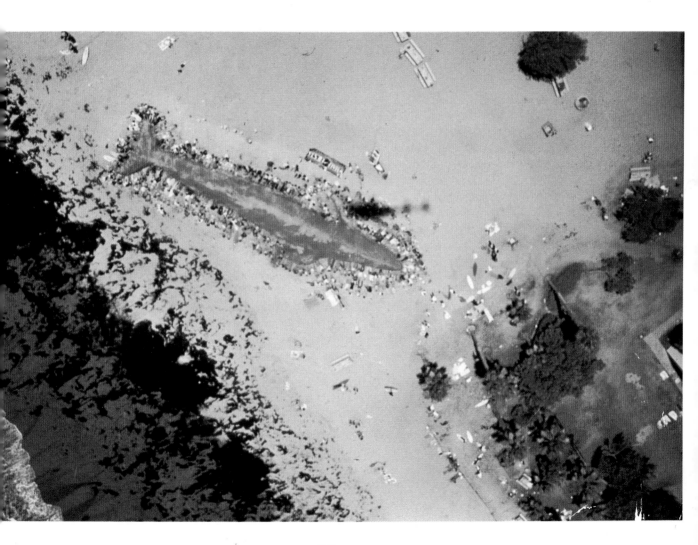

31

In December through February of each year herds of California gray whales make their way from the icy waters of the Arctic to the warm lagoons of Mexico. There the mother whales give birth to their young and mate again to create new life. In spring the herd moves northward, headed toward summer feeding grounds in the Arctic. The whales will have covered more than 10,000 miles during their round trip. Each year since 1974 thousands of Southern California school children have been given the opportunity to observe this amazing migration at first hand. Taking part in a program called "Whalewatch" (under the sponsorship of the Cabrillo Marine Museum and the American Cetacean Society), they are transported in specially chartered boats out into the Pacific for a closeup view of the whale herd's activities. In words and stunning color photographs the book *Whalewatch!* captures this fascinating experience for young boys and girls. The remarkable pictures graphically record almost every aspect of gray whale behavior and will give the reader a sense of having taken part in an actual whalewatch.

JUNE BEHRENS is the versatile author of nearly fifty books for young readers, ranging in subject matter from masterpieces of art and colonial history to zoo animals and the metric system. Her keen interest in wildlife conservation and the environment is nowhere better exemplified than in *Whalewatch!*, written from firsthand experience of an actual Whalewatch expedition. Mrs. Behrens has for many years been a reading specialist with one of California's largest public school systems. She has a Master's degree in Administration from the University of Southern California and holds a Credential in Early Childhood Education. She makes her home with her husband, a well-known educator, in Redondo Beach in Southern California.

JOHN OLGUIN, who is responsible for the many graphic photographs which illustrate *Whalewatch!*, is Director of the Cabrillo Marine Museum, located in San Pedro, California. The Museum is devoted to all types of marine life, from giant creatures of the deep to tiny seashells. It was Mr. Olguin who first conceived the idea of the highly successful Whalewatch program, a program which has enlightened and entertained many thousands of adults as well as children.